KIDS ON EARTH

Wildlife Adventures – Explore The World
Fruit Bat - Maldives

Sensei Paul David

COPYRIGHT PAGE

Kids On Earth: Wildlife Adventures - Explore The World

Fruit Bat - Maldives

by Sensei Paul David,

Copyright © 2023.

All rights reserved.

978-1-77848-201-4 KoE_WildLife_Amazon_PaperbackBook_maldives_fruit bat

978-1-77848-200-7 KoE_WildLife_Amazon_eBook_maldives_fruit bat

978-1-77848-430-8 KoE_Wildlife_Ingram_Paperbackbook_FruitBat Paperback

This book is not authorized for free distribution copying.

www.senseipublishing.com

@senseipublishing
#senseipublishing

Synopsis

This book provides an introduction to the fascinating world of fruit bats in the Maldives. It covers the two species that live there, the Black Flying Fox and the Small Flying Fox, and explores their behavior, diet, social structure, habitat, and more. It also looks at the important role they play in the ecosystem, their relationship with native plants, their hunting, and their importance to the local culture. This book is a great resource for those interested in learning more about the amazing fruit bats of the Maldives.

Get Our FREE Books Now!

kidsonearth.life

kidsonearth.world

Click Below for Another Book In Each Series

senseipublishing.com/KoE_SERIES

senseipublishing.com/KoE_Wildlife_SERIES

KoE En Español

senseipublishing.com/KoE_SERIES_SPANISH

www.senseipublishing.com

Join Our Publishing Journey!

If you would like to receive FUTURE FREE BOOKS and get to know us better, please click www.senseipublishing.com and join our newsletter by entering your email address in the pop-up box.

Follow Our Blog: senseipauldavid.ca

Follow/Like/Subscribe: Facebook, Instagram, YouTube: @senseipublishing

Scan the QR Code with your phone or tablet to follow us on social media:

Like / Subscribe / Follow

Introduction

Welcome to the fascinating world of fruit bats in the Maldives! These amazing creatures have a unique lifestyle, eating habits, and adaptations that make them so special. In this book, you'll learn all about their behavior, diet, social structure, and more. You'll also get to explore the habitats where these fruit bats live, from the lush and vibrant forests of the Maldives to the crystal clear waters of the Indian Ocean. So, let's get started!

Fruit bats are the only species of bats that feed on fruit, flowers, and nectar.

The Maldives is home to two species of fruit bats, the Black Flying Fox and the Small Flying Fox.

The Black Flying Fox can grow up to two feet in length and has a wingspan of nearly four feet.

The Small Flying Fox is much smaller, reaching only up to 9 inches in length and with a wingspan of 12 inches.

Fruit bats use their large ears to locate food sources, such as fruits and flowers.

They have an incredible sense of smell, which helps them to find food even in the dark.

Fruit bats live in large colonies and are highly social creatures, often forming close bonds with their kin.

The diet of fruit bats consists mainly of fruits, nectar, and pollen, and they can travel up to 10 miles in a single night in search of food.

Fruit bats are important pollinators of the Maldives' tropical forests.

Fruit bats have an impressive flying ability, using their large wings to maneuver with great agility.

Fruit bats have a unique way of drinking water, using their long tongues to lap up water from streams and lakes.

Fruit bats are nocturnal creatures and spend most of the day sleeping in trees or caves.

The Large Flying Fox is the largest fruit bat species in the world, with a wingspan of up to six feet.

Fruit bats use echolocation to navigate in the dark, sending out high-pitched sounds that bounce off of objects in their path.

The diet of fruit bats consists mainly of fruit, but they will also eat insects, leaves, and other vegetation.

Fruit bats are important seed dispersers, helping to spread the seeds of the fruit they eat throughout the forests of the Maldives.

The Small Flying Fox is an endangered species, with only a few thousand individuals left in the wild.

Fruit bats have a remarkable memory, able to remember where they find food sources even after months of absence.

The Black Flying Fox is a threatened species, with its population declining due to hunting and habitat destruction.

Fruit bats are a keystone species, playing an important role in maintaining the balance of the ecosystem in the Maldives.

The Maldives is home to several species of fruit bats, including the rare and elusive Red Flying Fox.

The Red Flying Fox feeds mainly on the nectar of flowers and is found only in the forests of the Maldives.

Fruit bats are a vital part of the food chain, providing food for a variety of predators such as owls, hawks, and snakes.

The Small Flying Fox has a unique courtship behavior, often circling around the female bat with its wings spread before mating.

The Large Flying Fox is the most common species of fruit bat in the Maldives, with a population of around 200,000 individuals.

The Black Flying Fox is the only species of fruit bat in the Maldives that migrates, travelling to Sri Lanka and India during the winter months.

Fruit bats have a unique relationship with the native plants of the Maldives, often playing a crucial role in pollination and seed dispersal.

Fruit bats are an important part of the culture in the Maldives, often featured in art, literature, and folklore.

Fruit bats are important for the health of the forests of the Maldives, as they help to spread the seeds of the fruit they eat.

Fruit bats are an important part of the local economy, as they are hunted for their meat and used in traditional medicine.

Conclusion

Fruit bats are an important species in the Maldives, playing a vital role in the local ecology and economy. They have a unique lifestyle, diet, and adaptations that make them so special, and they are an important part of the culture in the Maldives. So, the next time you're in the Maldives, don't forget to keep an eye out for these amazing and fascinating creatures!

Thank you for reading this book!

If you found this book helpful, I would be grateful if you would **post an honest review on Amazon** so this book can reach other supportive readers like you!

All you need to do is digitally flip to the back and leave your review. Or visit amazon.com/author/senseipauldavid click the correct book cover and click on the blue link next to the yellow stars that say, "customer reviews."

As always...

It's a great day to be alive!

Share Our FREE eBooks Now!

kidsonearth.life

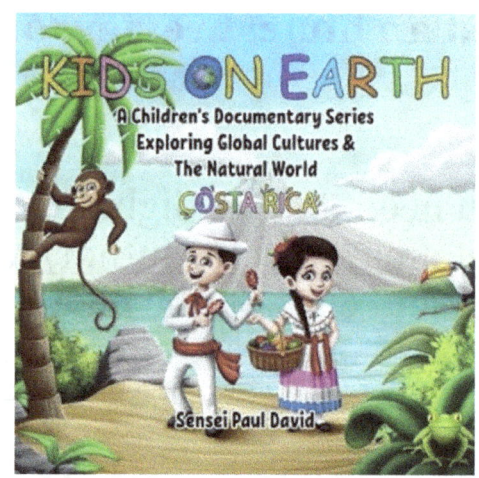

kidsonearth.world

Click Below for Another Book In Each Series

senseipublishing.com/KoE_SERIES   senseipublishing.com/KoE_Wildlife_SERIES

KoE En Español

senseipublishing.com/KoE_SERIES_SPANISH

www.senseipublishing.com

www.senseipublishing.com

@senseipublishing
#senseipublishing

Check out our **recommendations** for other books for adults & kids plus other great resources by visiting
www.senseipublishing.com/resources/

Join Our Publishing Journey!

If you would like to receive FREE BOOKS and special offers, please visit www.senseipublishing.com and join our newsletter by entering your email address in the pop-up box

Follow Our Engaging Blog NOW!
senseipauldavid.ca

Get Our FREE Books Today!

Click & Share the Links Below

FREE Kids Books

lifeofbailey.senseipublishing.com
kidsonearth.senseipublishing.com

FREE Self-Development Book

senseiselfdevelopment.senseipublishing.com

FREE BONUS!!!
Experience Over 25 FREE Engaging Guided Meditations!

Prized Skills & Practices for Adults & Kids. Help Restore Deep Sleep, Lower Stress, Improve Posture, Navigate Uncertainty & More.

Download the Free Insight Timer App and click the link below:
http://insig.ht/sensei_paul

About Sensei Publishing

Sensei Publishing commits itself to helping people of all ages transform into better versions of themselves by providing high-quality and research-based self-development books with an emphasis on mental health and guided meditations. Sensei Publishing offers well-written e-books, audiobooks, paperbacks, and online courses that simplify complicated but practical topics in line with its mission to inspire people toward positive transformation.

It's a great day to be alive!

About the Author

I create simple & transformative eBooks & Guided Meditations for Adults & Children proven to help navigate uncertainty, solve niche problems & bring families closer together.

I'm a former finance project manager, private pilot, jiu-jitsu instructor, musician & former University of Toronto Fitness Trainer. I prefer a science-based approach to focus on these & other areas in my life to stay humble & hungry to evolve. I hope you enjoy my work and I'd love to hear your feedback.

- It's a great day to be alive!
Sensei Paul David

Scan & Follow/Like/Subscribe: Facebook, Instagram, YouTube: @senseipublishing

Scan using your phone/iPad camera for Social Media
Visit us at www.senseipublishing.com and sign up for our newsletter to learn more about our exciting books and to experience our FREE Guided Meditations for Kids & Adults.

www.ingramcontent.com/pod-product-compliance
Lightning Source LLC
Chambersburg PA
CBHW080615110526
44587CB00040BB/3725